Star

Pie

by Sharon Tregenza
Illustrated by Irene Montano

OXFORD

UNIVERSITY PRESS

Chapter 1
The last of the bread

Long ago, on a stormy winter's day, a huge wave hit an old stone wall. Salty spray flew across the harbour and rattled the windows of Tom Bawcock's cottage.

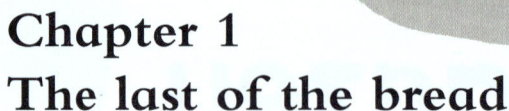

Tom's mother looked out across the wind-whipped sea. "Will this storm never end?" she said. "<u>Unless</u> the fishing boats go out to sea soon, we'll all starve. We have no fish to eat. I have nothing to put in my pies."

The fishing boats go out to sea every day <u>unless</u> the weather is bad. Why haven't the boats been out for a while?

"Everyone knows that you make the best pies in the village," Tom said. He was trying to cheer his mother up. "I like your special pies the best, and I like the funny names you give them. I remember you made a Puffy Cloud pie, a Bird in the Tree pie and a …"

BOOM!

Another wave crashed against the harbour wall. As Tom and his mother watched through the window, Tom's mother sighed. "We will have to make do with bread. There will be no pies for us tonight."

"If only I could make one quick trip out in my boat, I might be able to catch some fish," Tom thought.

Supper was a sad meal. Tom's mother divided the last of the bread between Tom and his younger brothers. She took the smallest piece for herself.

It broke Tom's heart to see his family go hungry.

Tom wished he could do something. It wasn't just his family that was suffering. The whole village was hungry.

When his mother and brothers were asleep, Tom got out of bed. He watched the angry sea break against the harbour wall. The <u>regular</u> beat of the waves echoed through the darkness.

A <u>regular</u> beat is where beats happen with the same space between them, in a steady rhythm. Can you clap, tap, or use your voice to make a <u>regular</u> beat, like the waves against the harbour wall?

Then, all at once, the wind dropped. The clouds began to part, and the moon and stars came out. "It's now or never," Tom thought. He sneaked out of the house and crept down to the harbour.

Chapter 2
Cast off

Tom climbed into his little boat. He grabbed the oars, took a deep breath … and started to row.

The moon was high up in the dark, inky sky. Tom rowed out of the harbour silently, with long, smooth strokes.

Tom went <u>directly</u> to his favourite spot to fish. He dropped the hook and line into the water. He soon caught a fish … then another and another. Before long, he was knee-deep in seven sorts of fish. Their scales glittered like jewels.

If Tom went <u>directly</u> to his favourite spot, does that mean he went there straight away, or went somewhere else first?

Tom was so excited by this stroke of luck that he forgot the first rule of fishing: always listen to the wind.

It started with a murmur and a whisper. Then there was a whistle and a whine.

Tom carried on fishing. At first, he didn't notice the wind blowing the water into waves. Then clouds blocked out the moon. The wind tore at Tom's clothes and tugged at his hair. It whipped salt water into his eyes.

The waves grew. Now Tom rode a wild and raging sea. The boat rolled one way and then the other. Tom held tightly to the sides.

Suddenly, lightning ripped a zigzag pattern across the dark sky.

The boat rose on the crest of one huge wave.

Then it dropped ... so suddenly it rattled all of Tom's teeth and bones.

The little boat pitched up and down and side to side. Thunder boomed. Lightning flashed. Tom was soaked by icy, salty waves.

All through the night, Tom fought against the storm to save his catch of fish.

At last, as the pale-grey dawn appeared, Tom knew that he had won.

He fell into a deep,

deep,

sleep.

Chapter 3
The feast

Tom woke with the warmth of the sun on his face. Seagulls flew above him. Their wings were a flash of white against the light-blue sky.

In the distance, Tom saw the harbour walls. While he had slept, his little boat had carried him home.

Then Tom heard shouts of joy. The whole village was waiting for him at the harbour.

Tom waved. His mother must have woken early and come out to look for him. He felt a stab of guilt as he realized how worried she must have been.

Tom's mother hugged him tight and said, "I should be cross, Tom. You could have drowned. The truth is, I'm very proud of you. It was a brave thing to do, and just look at all the fish! Tonight, we'll have a feast, for I shall make the biggest pie I've ever made."

Tom's mother says, "The truth is, I'm very proud of you." Can you think of other words she could have used instead of 'the truth is'?

Tom patted the side of his little wooden boat. He thanked it for keeping him safe.

Then Tom went home, changed out of his salt-soaked clothes and took a long, warm bath.

Tom's mother cleaned and cooked the seven sorts of fish.

That night, she made a pie large enough for everyone to share … a pie with fish gazing up at the stars.

The hungry villagers <u>accepted</u> it gratefully.

Can you pretend to be the hungry villagers, gratefully <u>accepting</u> the pie? What would you say to Tom and his mother?

"I shall call it Stargazey Pie," Tom's mother said. "I'll make it every year. Then everyone will remember the time young Tom Bawcock went to sea and saved the village from going hungry."

Tom's mother says, "I shall call it Stargazey Pie." Does this mean that she will call it Stargazey Pie, or not?

Read and discuss

Read and talk about the following questions.

Page 3: <u>Unless</u> you get distracted, reading a book can be a good way to relax. What kinds of things could distract you from reading?

Page 7: What do you do at a <u>regular</u> time each day or each week?

Page 10: If you travel <u>directly</u> from your house to your school, how long does it take?

Page 20: Tell a partner two <u>truths</u> about yourself and one lie. Can they guess which is the lie?

Page 22: Can you think of some things that you might <u>accept</u> gratefully?

Page 23: 'I <u>shall</u> go to the park,' means, 'I will go the park.' Try to make a statement about what you will do later, starting with: *I <u>shall</u>* …